Chittor
(Chittaurgarh)

An Overview of Chittor

CHITTOR

(CHITTAURGARH)

Historical View and a Guide

Irmgard Meininger

D.K. Printworld (P) Ltd.
New Delhi - 110015

Cataloging in Publication Data — DK

Meininger, Irmgard, 1947 –
Chittor: historical view and a guide.
Includes bibliographical references (p.).

1. Chittorgarh (India) — History. 2. Chittorgarh (India) — Description and travel. 3. Mewar, House of — History. 4. Rajasthan (India) — Kings and rulers. 5. Rajasthan (India) — History. I. Title.

ISBN - 81-246-0150-X

First published in India in 2000

Published and printed by:
D.K. Printworld (P) Ltd.
Regd. office: '*Sri Kunj*', F-52, Bali Nagar
New Delhi - 110 015
Phone: (011) 545-3975, 546-6019; *Fax*: (011) 546-5926
E-mail: dkprint@4mis.com

Brian Masters
47, Caithness Road
London W14 6JD

Foreword

It is now ten years since I wrote a history of the ruling family of Mewar, sitting on a terrace at Shivniwas Palace and typing out an astonishing saga which covered fourteen centuries and which gave the Indian sub-continent both its greatest hero, Rana Pratap, and its most illustrious man of letters and patron of the arts, Maharana Kumbha. Working from ancient documents translated for me by a venerable sage who had devoted his life to the family, there unfolded before me a story so stirring that my enthusiasm grew with each discovery, and by the end I felt as much pride in these people as if I had been a Hindu myself.

Perhaps the greatest moment was when I was driven to Chittor, which had been the mighty capital of Mewar for 800 years from its foundation in 734. It was a magical place of impressive dimensions, so frowning at the horizon that one could well imagine the enemy's trepidation as its walls loomed a head. And despite its having been laid waste in the sixteenth century, the stones still hummed with distant memories of real inhabitants. The ruins afforded me the same tingling pleasure which is generally provoked by the ancient Roman Forum, and not far below the surface upon which I trod, a layer of human ash testified to the people's amazing hold on their honour.

Irmgard Meininger has rendered a signal service to all of us with this splendid account of the city, illustrated with such taste and devotion that dignity is triumphantly restored to a vanished past.

Preface

This guidebook is dedicated to the people of Mewar, the descendants of different tribes of Bhils and to the present custodian of the Royal House of Mewar, Shriji Arvind Singhji Mewar in commemoration of bold, brave, and selfless sacrifice of lives by not only the rulers of Mewar and their wives but also by other men and women of Chittor.

It is written for all visitors of Rajasthan, Indians as well as foreign tourists, first curious to see and then understand this important place of Indian history and culture, with the hope that they will engage themselves in a better preservation of this sacred place.

It is also meant to arouse the Indian Government to do all that is necessary to protect this important and sacred place of Indian history. It is also hoped that the work will interest members of the UNESCO so that Chittor may be recognised as a 'World Heritage Object' just as the most important buildings of the Mughal Emperors of India are under-protection of the UNESCO and therefore well-maintained.

Kirti Stambha

Contents

Chittor in the Eyes of Historians and Travellers

Strolling round through the wind-blown ruins of the temples and palaces,
the history, written of blood and fire,
suddenly seems to be frightening present.

— Thomas Barkemeier in *Rajasthan*
(translated by the author)

The history of Rajasthan is something marvellous
but the history of Chittor is above everything.
Three times in its history the women never turned their backs
when they saw their husbands were losing.
Either they went into the battlefield
wearing men's clothes and sacrificed themselves
or they entered the pyre and threw their children
on the pyre so as not to surrender to the intruders.
Even girls of fifteen went out fighting or went into the fire.
It is awe-inspiring to think of it.
Even today when you go to Chittor you feel it.
It is our holiest of holies and yet in every nook and cranny in the land
you'll find there were brave people who made great sacrifices.

— Maharani of Wankaner, sister of the Maharawal of Dungapur
(also descendants of Bapa Rawal)
in Charles Allen: *Lives of the Indian Princes*

The funeral Pyre was lighted within the great subterranean retreat
in chambers impervious to the light of day,
and the defenders of Chittor beheld in procession
the queens, their own wives, and daughters
to the number of several thousands.
The fair Padmini closed the throng.

They were conveyed to the cavern, and the opening closed up upon them leaving them to find security from dishonour in the devouring element....

The Rana, satisfied that his line was not extinct,
now prepared to follow his brave sons;
and calling around him his devoted clans,
they threw open the portals and descended to the plains,
and with reckless despair carried death,
or met it, in the crowded ranks of Ala.

— Colonel James Tod in *Annals and Antiquities of Rajasthan*, Vol. 1

CHITORGARH
From times when forth from the sunlight
The first of our kings came down,
And had the earth for his footstool
And wore the stars for his crown.

A still silence hangs over the deserterd pavilions
and ruined temples of Chitorgarh.
Three times in its history, the Sisodia princes of Mewar led their warriors
from its walls to carry death to the besiegers or meet it in the field.
Three times they left behind them the terrible johar,
the voluntary immolation of their women and children.
Death for all before dishonour.

— Virginia Fass in *The Forts of India*

On the plateau of a long narrow solitary hill rising 180 metres
above the flat plains 112 km north-east of Udaipur
stands the ghostly remains of Chittorgarh,
the greatest of all Rajasthan's fortified citadels.
No other place evokes the Rajput's spirit
of chivalry, courage, romance, and passion.
As is the case with places of exceptional greatness,
it is assumed that Chittorgarh has mythological origins

— Kim Naylor in *Discovery Guide to Rajasthan*

She (Padmini) was the fairest of all flesh on the earth.
Her fame was sung through the land by the poets,
and she became, in some sort
the Helen of Chittor.

— Rudyard Kipling in *Letter of Marque*

It was said that this fort (Chittor) was the key to all of Rajputana,
and any conqueror who had ambitions on Rajputana
had to first wrest control of it.
It is considered by many to be the finest medieval Hindu fort in existence.
But more than that,
it is cloaked in legends of valor, chivalry, and glorious death
and occupies a pre-eminent position in the Rajput psyche.

— Anjula Bedi *et al.* in *Rajasthan* (Everyman's Guide)

The leading Rajput power was the state of Mewar, led by Udai Singh
(r. 1537-72) who proudly scorned any dealings with the new rulers of Delhi.
In 1568 Akbar laid siege to Udai Singh's capital of Chittor,
a vast rocky crag in the middle of the desert.
After a fierce struggle the fortress was captured
but there was to be no surrender.
As was their custom,
the Rajput preferred death for all before dishonour.
In a terrible ritual known as the 'Jauhar',
the women and children threw themselves into the flames of funeral pyre
while the men sallied out to fight to the death.
All the Rajput warriors duly died in the ensuing battle.
Those who survived the holocaust, some 30,000 or so,
were massacred on Akbar's order as warning to others. . . .
Its (Chittor's) ruins are still an awesome sight today:
one of the finest surviving examples of medieval Hindu fortifications,
its walls tower some 500 feet above the plain.
A still silence hang over the walls, the deserted pavilions
and the ruined temples —
the brooding memory of a savage past.

— Sindharaja Tammita-Delgoda in
A Traveller's History of India

The armourers of the Rajputs, the Gadi Lohars,
whose traditional home was Chittor,
are today wandering tribe.
Once they produced top quality weapons and armour for their masters.
After the fall of Chittor to Akbar in 1567,
they swore never to return to the citadel
until it was freed.
In the early 1950s, Pandit Nehru
personally led them back to a free Chittor,
but their nomadic habits were too deeply ingrained in them.

— E. Jaiwant Paul in *By my Sword and Shield*

Historical Overview

Chittor, also called Chittaurgarh, is a place with such a unique history and situation that you will not find any comparable place in the world. The sentence of Barkemeier might astonish those, who have no knowledge about the history of Chittor and the Kingdom of Mewar. But those who know about its history will also be struck with we while visiting this sacred place.

The fort of Chittor is situated on a 170 m high table hill, about 450 m above sea level, with deep declivities on all sides. The narrow hill has an extension from north to south of almost 5 km and is very small from west to east. It measures 280 ha.

Chittor, was the capital of the rulers of Mewar from the eighth until the sixteenth century. The House of Mewar is the world's oldest ruling dynasty which now spans 76 generations and about 1500 years.

The name derives from the founder, King Chitrangad Maurya (Mori). The last ruler of the Maurya at Chittor was Raja

Overview Over a Part of Chittor

Man Mori, an uncle of Bapa Rawal, who is the real founder of the Kingdom of Mewar and the ancestor of all Maharanas of Mewar (today, Udaipur).

The Royal Family of Mewar can trace its pedigree back to the sixth century in the territory of Mewar. But the origin of the family at Idar is even centuries older. Mewar is the most respected Rajput clan of India, now called the clan of 'Sisodias', in former times the 'Guhilots'.

The 'Sisodias of Mewar' are well-known for their spirit of self-respect and respect for other thinking and believing human beings, but especially for their heroic resistance against all Turkish, Afghan, and other Muslim aggressors.

The history of Mewar is the history of heroic men and women to whom their honour, religion, and freedom were always much more important than their lives.

The history of the House of Mewar is rooted in mythology going into and beyond the realm of recorded history. The Rulers of Mewar trace their descent back to Lav and the sun. Lav is one of the sons of the Lord Rama, whose history is recorded in the famous epic the *Ramayana*. Therefore, the Royal Family has the sun in its crest.

The inscription means:

The Crest of Mewar

The Almighty protects those who stand steadfast in upholding righteousness.

The first ancestor about whom we know some historical facts is Guhil. In AD 525 the former capital of the family at Valabhibas was sacked by invaders while the pregnant Queen Pushpavati was on pilgrimage to the shrine of the universal mother Amba-Bhavani in her native land. The whole royal family was erased except the queen and her unborn son. When she got the horrible news on her way back, she took refuge with a Brahmin priest and his daughter in a cave of the Aravalli Hills until her son was born. She gave him the name Guhil (cave born) and confided the baby to the daughter of the Brahmin priest with the instruction to care for and educate the prince as a Brahmin. Then she mounted the funeral pyre and burned herself to join her murdered husband.

Guhil was a very wild child who spent most of his time during the day with persons of the native race of the Bhils and became a favourite with their chieftain. When the Bhils had decided to elect a king, their choice fell on Guhil. For the coronation the chieftain of the Bhils cut his thumb and applied his blood as the *tika* of sovereignty upon the forehead of Guhil.

The capital of Guhil and his successors until the time of the real founder of the Kingdom of Mewar, Kalbhoj, later known as Bapa Rawal, was Nagda, named after the fourth ruler, Nagaditya.

Very little is known about the following six rulers. The seventh ruler, Mahendra II died in AD 734 in a hunting accident. His son, Kalbhoj, the later founder of the Kingdom of Mewar, was only three years old that time. Again a Brahmin, a descendant of the Brahmin who had protected Guhil, took care of the little prince and conveyed him to a fortress where he was protected by two Bhils of another tribe. With them he looked after the cows. One fine day the 'royal cowboy' met Sage Harit Rishi of the Lakulish Cult who was a great devotee of Lord Shiva. He told the sage all he knew about himself and received his blessings.

From the first meeting, Kalbhoj visited the sage daily to wash his feet, carry milk to him and gather wild flowers for the deity. In return Harit Rishi gave him lessons in morality and introduced him into the mysterious rites of Lord Eklingji (Shiva). Finally, he bestowed the State of Mewar on his pupil and laid down the cardinal duties as guiding principles for service to the State for Bapa Rawal (Kalbhoj) and all his successors:

1. To follow the eternal principles of *Manav Dharma* (Religion of Man) and preserve and perpetuate 'Vedic Culture'.
2. To serve all God's Creations as a service to God, the Creator of All Life.
3. To constantly endeavour to keep the human soul awakened and alive, in order that human beings would value the 'Dignity of Man'.
4. To help recognise Man's special status in the hierarchy of God's creations — the eternal principles underlying cosmic creation.
5. There shall be no distinction nor any discrimination in the service of Man, and it shall not be limited by either space or time.
6. All things belong to God, as such, the State of Mewar be considered as belonging to Shree Eklingji and the Maharanas were to hold the State as a sacred Trust and perform all duties and obligations as the 'Diwan' (Representative or Prime Minister) of Shree Eklingji.

Later, Bapa Rawal met another sage, the famed Goraknath, who gave him the double-edged sword which could sever even rocks. At this time Chittor was ruled by Raja Man Mori of Maurya, an uncle from the side of Bapa's mother. During his reign the first Afghan invaders came to Rajputana. Most of the Rajput clans moved with their warriors to Chittor, to fight together against the new enemy. When the Afghans laid siege to Chittor all Rajput

Bapa Rawal Receives the State of Mewar as a Blessing

leaders held a great council. Raja Man Mori and a lot of other leaders thought of surrendering the fort, because they had recognised that the army of the Afghans was much larger and had better arms. But Bapa was convinced that the enemy had to be conquered and he led those Rajput forces who trusted in him against the Afghans.

Bapa defeated the enemy and his uncle abdicated and proposed Bapa as the better leader and king. So, he was elected by all Rajput chiefs as their king and the Bhils also elected him as their new paramount chief. His two Bhils companions applied the *tika* of sovereignty on his forehead, just like the Bhil chief had done to Guhil about 200 years ago.

Bapa built the first temple at Eklingji which is till now the personal deity temple of the Royal Family of Mewar and temples in Chittor. Historians say that he built the temple at the place where we find the temple of Kalika Mata today.

He was an absolutely extraordinary personality: he — the real founder of this unique kingdom — established the seat of administration at Chittor and Chittor remained the capital of Mewar for about eight hundred years; he had plenty of wives, Hindus, daughters of Isphahan, Kandahar, Kashmir, Iran, Iraq, etc. 98 Hindu children, called *'Agni-upasi Suryavansi'* (sun born fire-worshippers), and 130 other sons, called 'Nasshahra Pathans'. He ruled from AD 734 to 753, and then retired to become a *samnyasi*. When he died he had reached the patriarchal age of 100 years.

All subsequent Rulers of Mewar are descendants of the blood of Bapa Rawal.

The successors of Bapa enlarged the territory of the State and had no 'real problems' with foreign aggressors, which means that there was no existential danger to the State of Mewar until the reign of Ratan Singh who succeeded to the *gaddi* (throne) in AD 1302. Of course, there were a lot of battles and wars as a result of attacks by Afghan invaders, who sacked many other Rajput

States. Colonel James Tod writes about the forty-first ruler, Samar Singh (AD 1273-1302), in his famous *Annals and Antiquities of Rajasthan*:

> Mewar alone, the sacred bulwark of religion, never compromised her honour for her safety, and still survives her ancient limits; and since the brave Samarsi gave up his life, the blood of her princes has flowed in copious streams for the maintenance of this honour, religion and independence.

At the time of death of Samar Singh, the Muslim ruler Ala-ud Din had become a great danger for all Rajput States. He attacked Gujarat in 1299 and conquered the fort of Ranthambor in AD 1299-1300. He further thought of subduing Chittor and Malwa also for military and personal reasons. The possession of Chittor seemed to him helpful for his planned expansions to wards Central India. The successor of Samar was his son Ratan. The younger brother, Kumbh Karan Singh left Rajasthan and went to Nepal.

Ala-ud Din had heard about the breathtaking beauty of the Queen of Chittor, the wife of Ratan. Ratan had married a princess of Ceylon with the name Padmini. Going by all the inscriptions of those days she must have been an extraordinary beauty. Ala-ud Din wished to get this beautiful queen for his harem.

In AD 1302, only a few months after the accession of Ratan, Ala-ud Din and his army attacked Chittor for two months without

The Water Pavilion of Padmini

The Mardana of Padmini's Palace

success. Many of the Muslim soldiers died not only in the fighting but also in epidemics and floods.

Regarding the events that followed, historians are not of the same opinion. Fact is that, Ratan invited Ala-ud Din to a meeting in Chittor, probably with the intention of making an honourable treaty. Historians record that Ala-ud Din saw the beautiful Rani (Queen) Padmini in a mirror of the *mardana* while she was on the steps of her water pavillon, which was surrounded by water.

He demanded Padmini as a price for the liberty of Chittor. Of course, Ratan refused, but as a chivalrous king he did not throw Ala-ud Din into prison but escorted him to the gates of Chittor. There Ratan was kidnapped and the price for his freedom was the delivering of Rani Padmini.

Ala-ud Din was excited when he heard she would come to him to save the life of her husband but under the condition that she could bring her court ladies with her. Of course, this was a ruse. When the brave Padmini left the citadel to be brought to the camp of the enemy there were under the cover of the palanquins the best Rajput warriors led by Gora and Badal (an uncle and a cousin of

The Room with Mirrors

Padmini) instead of court ladies. In the battle Rana Ratan and Rani Padmini could escape, but most of the Rajput warriors were killed. Because, the Muslims too had suffered heavy losses, Ala-ud Din was obliged to retire.

In AD 1303, he returned with a large army to Chittor. When Ratan realised that he had no chance of defeating the large Muslim army, he smuggled his nephew Ari Singh out of Chittor in safety for the survival of his royal house.

Padmini, the beautiful queen, preferred death to dishonour. She ordered a large funeral pyre be lit in the cellars of Chittor, and led all noble Rajput ladies, dressed in their wedding clothes and decorated with their jewels, together with all noble children to the vast funeral pyre, where they burned themselves. After the death of their women and children Ratan and his Rajput warriors — dressed in their saffron robes — rushed out of the fortress to fight to the finish. When Ala-ud Din entered the fort and recognised what had happened, he was so angry that he gave the order for a general massacre of the civil population of lower castes who had not sacrificed their lives. About 30,000 persons were slaughtered on his order and he demolished all buildings, palaces, and temples. He only spared the water pavilion of Padmini.

This was the first *jauhar* and *sakka* of Chittor.

Mewar had the good fortune that the son of Ari Singh, Hamir, became one of the greatest rulers of medieval India. Hamir succeeded to the titles after the death of his father in AD 1314 and ruled — first staying at Kelawara — from AD 1326 to 1364. He continually fought battles against the Muslims and consolidated his power.

Hamir was a great military leader as well as a great diplomat. He was able to recapture Chittor, and extended the power of Mewar through a lot of successful battles. As a result of his successes, the rulers of Mewar affirmed their supremacy over all other Rajput dynasties and since his times the ruler of Mewar alone is recognised as Rana or Maharana while all other rulers wear only the title Raja or Maharaja (the pre-fix *maha* means 'great'). He rebuilt the former temple of the Sun God, built by Bapa Rawal, and placed an image of Kalika, the patron goddess of Chittor, to replace that of the Sun God and named the temple Kalika Mata Temple.

Hamir's grandson, Maharana Lakha (AD 1382-1421) continued to erect beautiful palaces and wonderful temples at Chittor and by developing zinc and silver mines as important sources of revenue to the State, he achieved great prosperity. It is said that he laid the foundation for the long tradition of the now world-wide recognised Mewar painting.

Kalika Mata Temple

One of the greatest rulers not only of Mewar but also of the whole medieval India was Maharana Kumbha, who succeeded to the *gaddi* of Mewar in AD 1433.

It is quite unbelievable that he would not have been born without a joke of his grandfather Maharana Lakha. The story is quite amusing despite its serious consequences for the royal families of Mewar and Marwar (Jodhpur). When Maharana Lakha was already an old man, Rao Ranmal, the ruler of the clan of Rathores in Mandore (Marwar), wanted to marry his sister Hansabai to Lakha's eldest son, Chunda Singh. Dhananjaya Singh, a descendant of Marwar, writes:

> The Sisodias of Mewar, like the Rathores, are Suryavanshi Rajputs claiming solar descendance from Lord Rama, but enjoy the pre-eminent position amongst all the Hindu clans of India. Marriage alliances with the House of Mewar, by far the oldest in Rajputana, have been fervently sought down the ages and this particular one, the first reported Rathore-Sisodia alliance, was significant for it reflected the rising star of a newcomer.

Corresponding to a medieval Rajput custom, the ceremony of engagement was performed with the presentation of a coconut to the bridegroom (a symbol for the honest desire for a marriage). When the ambassador from Marwar came with the ceremonial coconut, prince Chunda was absent. So Maharana Lakha received the messenger courteously and joked, "*I don't suppose you send such playthings to an old greybeard like me!*" When Chunda came back and heard about this event, he refused to accept the symbol and to marry Hansabai (Mewar historians are convinced that he was a faithful son who had refused because he had recognised that his father would like to marry the princess himself). However, Lakha could not return the symbol without gross insult to the house of Marwar and the princess. So he decided to marry Hansabai himself and made the condition that Chunda should renounce his right of primogeniture to the throne of Mewar. Chunda swore on Eklingji to fulfil his father's wishes: not only to renounce his right to the *gaddi* but also to be for his lifetime a guardian of the State. The old Rana and Hansabai got a son, Mokal. When Lakha died in AD 1421, Chunda kept his promise, refused the throne, and demonstrated his allegiance to his young half-brother. Because Hansabai became jealous and feared the influence of Chunda, he left Chittor with his other brothers, except his brother Raghavadeva, whom he left in Chittor, to keep an eye on all activities which could be against the interest of Mewar, including the Rathores whom he did not trust.

Maharana Mokal was assassinated in AD 1433 by Cacha and Mera, two illegitimate sons of his grandfather Kheta Singh.

At the time of his succession, Maharana Kumbha was still a minor and the sovereignty of the House of Mewar was in great danger: one of the murderers of Mokal wished to proclaim himself as Rana; at the same time the Muslim rulers of Malwa and Gujarat wanted to occupy Chittor and Rao Ranmal of Mandore came with his son Jodha (the later founder of Jodhpur) and a large army to Chittor, officially to protect his grand-nephew Kumbha, but in reality to annex Mewar. Raghavadeva, the younger brother of Chunda, soon realised the intentions of Rao Ranmal. When he raised protest he was murdered insidiously. The fair Chunda returned to Chittor to liberate it for his step-brother Kumbha from the Rathores. Ranmal became a victim of the revenge of a woman and his own weakness for wine, women, and opium. Chunda managed to get into the fort. Rao Ranmal and many of his followers were killed in one night and thus the Rathore interference in Mewar came to an end. The description by Colonel James Tod of the end of Rao Ranmal shows, that it was more ridiculous than tragical:

> Smitten with the charms of a Sisodia handmaid of the queen, who was compelled to his embrace, the old chief was in her arms, intoxicated with love, wine, and opium, and heard nothing of the tumult without. A woman's wit and revenge combined to make his end afford some compensations for her loss of honour. Gently rising, she bound him to his bed with his own Marwari turban: nor did this disturb him, and the messengers of fate had entered ere the opiate allowed his eyes to open to a sense of his danger. Enraged, he in vain endeavoured to extricate himself; and by some tortuosity of movement he got upon his legs, his pallet at his back like a shell or shield of defence. With no arms but a brass vessel of ablution he levelled to the earth several of his assailants, when a ball from a matchlock extended him on the floor of the palace.

After overcoming the difficulties in his youth, Maharana Kumbha became the greatest ruler of medieval India. He was an excellent general who defeated a number of Muslim Sultans and extended the territory of Mewar to an enormous size. In

Facing page: Vijaya Stambha

Palace of Kumbha in Chittor

commemoration of his victory over Mahmud Khalji of Malwa in AD 1437 he erected the Vijaya Stambha (tower of victory) at Chittor.

He was also a great statesman, who recognised that he needed not only brave warriors but also capable administrators. He was the first who appointed Prime Ministers who were no Sisodias. From Maharana Kumbha up to the time of Maharana Fateh Singh seven Prime Ministers belonged to the Kothari family, now living in Udaipur.

And he was a great sponsor of all kinds of arts. Everywhere in Mewar you will find witnesses of his great architectural activities: he built 32 forts, such as the fort of Kumbhalgarh which is named after him, and he sponsored the construction of the beautiful marble carved Jain temples at Ranakpur. Kumbha, who, reigned over the State of Mewar for a long period of 35 years (AD 1433-68) was a great scholar and musician and the author of several books.

This great Maharana died by the hand of a murderer. The murderer was his eldest son, Udai I, who was too impatient to wait for the throne. Udai could only enjoy a very short reign as the ruler of Mewar. The nobles of Mewar, who did not tolerate the assassination of the great Kumbha, took advantage of a timely absence of Udai and crowned his younger brother Raimal as King of Mewar. On his escape, Udai was struck down by a flash of a lightning.

Maharana Kumbha

The succession of Raimal (AD 1473-1509) was not free of problems. The two brothers of the eldest son and the heir-apparent (after the common right of primogeniture) tried to kill their elder brother, Sangram, later called 'The Mighty Sanga'. But Sanga survived the attack, losing one eye in the scuffle. He became another very great and important ruler of Mewar. Maharana Sanga (AD 1509 -27) was, as Virginia Fass writes in *The Forts of India*, "adored by his people, admired by his nobles", and he was the first and only ruler in northern India who was able to unite nearly all Rajput forces, for example, of the houses of Amber (later Jaipur), Marwar (Jodhpur), Gwalior, Ajmer, seven big rulers, nine Raos, and about 100 Rawats under his command. He also had 100,000 warriors and about 500 elephants besides the horses in his own army.

Sanga fought so successfully against Babur, the first Great Mughal, at Bayana, that Babur became demoralised and abjured the consumption of his beloved wine forever and also gave away all utensils like gold and silver cups and goblets. When the 'Mighty Sanga' died, it could be remarked that he had lost an eye

The Mighty Sanga

and an arm, possessed a crippled leg, having been broken by a cannon ball, and had eighty wounds from swords or lances on various parts of his body. Sanga appears to have been poisoned in AD 1527 by two of his nobles who were against his continued resistance towards the Mughals.

After the death of Sanga new problems for the State emerged as a result of the practice of polygamy which was common in those times. Sanga, who had 28 wives, had given a big *jagir* during his lifetime to his favourite wife, Karnavati, a Hada princess of Bundi, and her sons Vikramaditya and Udai because Karnavati feared that one of the elder sons and not one of her sons would become the successor of Sanga. The *jagir* consisted of the important fort of Ranthambor and the golden crown and belt which Maharana Kumbha had taken from Sultan Mahmud Khalji of Malwa. At the time of Sanga's death the eldest son Bhojraj, who was married to the famous poetess Mira Bai had already expired shortly after the marriage. Ratan II (AD 1527-31) then came to the *gaddi* of Mewar.

Ratan tried everything to get the Ranthambor fort and the jewels back. But he fell fighting with the brother of Rani Karnavati, Rao Surajmal Hada of Bundi, who also died in that single combat.

The new Maharana, Vikramaditya (AD 1531-36) had no qualities of a ruler. Colonel Tod writes about him in his famous *Annals and Antiquities of Rajasthan*:

> This prince had all the turbulence, without the redeeming qualities of character, which endeared his brother to his subjects; he was insolent, passionate, and vindictive, and utterly regardless of that respect which his proud nobles rigidly exacted. Instead of appearing at their head, he passed his time amongst wrestlers and prize-fighters, on whom and a multitude of 'paiks', or foot-soldiers, he lavished those gifts and that approbation, to which the aristrocratic Rajput, the equestrian order of Rajasthan, arrogated exclusive right.

Vikramaditya made so many mistakes that a lot of important chiefs left him. His sister-in-law, Mira Bai, who had not committed *sati* (self-burning of a widow on the cremation of her husband) had to face great hardship under him. She devoted her life to Lord Krishna in praise of whom she composed and sang her hymns. Vikramaditya, who found it scandalous for a Rani to confess her love to anybody else than her husband, even when it was a god, tried to take her life. After two attempts to kill her, she migrated to Medata in Marwar.

His mistakes in internal and external diplomacy and war strategy, resulted in an attack of the Sultan of Gujarat, Bahadur Shah. Rani Karnavati, who was conscious about the desolate situation and the great danger for the kingdom, brought about by her son, used an old Rajput tradition to get the help of the Great Mughal Humayun, the son of Babur. She sent him a *rakhi*-bracelet. Colonel Tod writes about *rakhi*:

> whatever its origin, it is one of the few when an intercourse of gallantry of the most delicate nature is established between the fair sex and the cavaliers of Rajasthan. Though, the bracelet may be sent by maidens, it is only on occasions of urgent necessity or danger. The Rajput dame bestows with the Rakhi the title of adopted brother; and while its acceptance secures to her all the protection of a cavalière servente; scandals ittself never suggests

A Rakhi Bracelet

> any other tie to his devotion. He may hazard his life in her cause, and yet never receive a smile in reward, for he cannot even see the fair object who, as brother of her adoption, has constituted him her defender. But there is a charm in the mystery of such a connexion, never endangered by close observation, and the loyalty to the fair may well attach a value to the public recognition of being the Rakhi-band Bhai, the 'bracelet-bound brother' of a princess.

Humayun left Bengal immediately to help his adopted sister, Karnavati, but he came too late. The brave queen clad herself in armour and fought on the battlefield. When she realised that there was no more hope to defend Chittor, she brought her sons Vikramaditya and Udai to safety and led all the noble women and children into the funeral pyre, like Padmini had done centuries ago.

About thirteen thousand women and children sacrificed their lives by burning themselves. The Rajput warriors opened the gates of Chittor again and rushed into their death, killing as many invaders as possible.

This was the second *jauhar* and *sakka* of Chittor which

happened in AD 1535. Humayun arrived too late to save the Queen Karnavati, but he defeated Bahadur Shah and gallantly reinstalled Vikramaditya as Maharana.

Vikramaditya, who had learned nothing from the devastating consequences of his earlier mistakes, continued in his old path. The council of the nobles of Mewar decided to replace him and installed Banbir, an illegitimate son of a brother of Sanga, as regent.

The choice was not a happy one at all, because Banbir killed Vikramaditya and also tried to kill Udai who was at that time a boy of six years. Udai was only saved by the brave and selfless sacrifice of his faithful nurse, Panna Dai, who had realised the situation and placed her own little son instead of Udai in the bed of the prince. She had to witness, the slaughter of her son by Banbir. After the cremation of her son she fled with Prince Udai to Kumbhalgarh, where he grew up as a nephew of the Prime Minister.

Years later, Udai was recognised by faithful nobles of Mewar as the real heir of Sanga and crowned. Udai defeated Banbir at Chittor and threw him and his family out without taking hard

The Fort of Kumbhalgarh

Maharana Udai Singh (1537-1573) - The Founder of Udaipur

revenge. He generously let the murderer of his brother, and the aggressor on his own life, leave Chittor with his family.

Meanwhile, Akbar, the mightiest of the Great Mughals, had extended his power and subjugated the greater part of northern India. Most of the other Rajput rulers, first of all Kanwar Man Singh and his father, Raja Bhagwant Das of Amber, had submitted and given Rajput ladies to Akbar's harem.

Only the House of Mewar was resistant. Udai refused to bow his head and to give up the independence of Mewar. When Akbar realised that he would not be able to subdue Mewar by a treaty, he planned to destroy the Kingdom of Mewar with the support of Kanwar Man Singh of Amber. The council of the nobles of Mewar decided that the Maharana and his sons should survive and leave Chittor. Maharana Udai II and his proud son, (Prince) Pratap, who later became one of the greatest heroes of Indian history, bowed after long discussions, their heads to this decision and left Chittor.

Before leaving Chittor, Udai gave the command of Chittor to Jaimal Rathore of Badnor and Patta of Kelwa, two young knights of only sixteen years of age. Akbar and Bhagwant Das of Amber laid siege to Chittor which lasted four months without real success. Then, an unhappy incident brought on the final fate of Chittor. Akbar was trying a new gun. When he saw a lone Rajput conducting repairs of a breach in the walls, he fired with his gun on that Rajput and the warrior tottered out of Akbar's sight. The lone Rajput was Jaimal himself and he was mortally wounded.

Recognising that it would not be possible to defeat Chittor without their chief and commander Jaimal, again the women, raised with the same standard of honour as the Rajput men, dressed themselves in their bridal clothes and lighted the funeral pyre in the cellars of Chittor. They preferred *jauhar* to the capture by an enemy army. Nine Ranis (queens), five princesses and all women and children of the nobles sacrificed their lives in the funeral pyre.

Next morning, Jaimal, who was seriously wounded and was carried by his clansman Kalla on his shoulders, and Patta, accompanied by his young bride and his mother, led the Rajput army into a glorious death. Patta, his bride, and his mother died fighting side by side.

This third and last *jauhar* or *sakka* happened in 1567. Jaimal and Patta are unforgotten heroes of Mewar. Even today, Jaimal and Patta are household names in Mewar.

When Akbar realised that he had neither killed the royal family nor got the treasures of Mewar, because they had been earlier brought away and hidden by the then Prime Minister, Bhamashah, he was so enraged that he ordered a 'holocaust'. Akbar was not only the tolerant and humane ruler is described by a lot of historians. On his command all the 30,000 surviving inhabitants, who did not belong to the warrior caste and had not been involved in the fights, were slain. And he vengefully did his utmost to destroy all buildings and works of art. If one is keen to excuse this awful deed of Akbar as a single derailment caused by his anger, he should know that this was not his only cruelty. Later, when Akbar conquered Gujarat, he gave the order to make a pyramid of 2000 heads of Hindus as deterrence.

A real and everlasting blot on the history of the House of Jaipur is the behaviour of Raja Bhagwant Das of Amber and his son, Kanwar Man Singh. They did not only support Akbar in the fights against their Hindu brothers and sisters, but even worse, they did nothing to try to hinder this barbaric massacre.

Udai Singh stayed with his family at Udaipur, Kumbhalgarh, and Gogunda, a village close to Udaipur and Udai Sagar, while the palace at Udaipur was under construction (AD 1559-64). Brian Masters writes in *Maharana*:

> Though Chittor was gone, the spirit of the Sisosdia clan did not go with it.

He was the only Rajput ruler who refused to bow his head to

Lakeside of the City Palace

Akbar. He not only built Udaipur but also prepared guerrilla attacks against the Mughals.

Udai Singh died on 28th February 1572 at Gogunda, leaving 25 sons and 20 queens.

The eldest son of Udai, Pratap Singh, became, after his succession to the throne, a legendary hero of Indian history:

> Maharana Pratap holds a unique position in the history of India. His unique example of combating the mighty Mughals, with a meagre man-power is rare in the history of the world. No one can be compared with the invincible Rana, who always held his head high amidst many vicissitudes of life (Suresh Goyal).

Pratap, who knew, of course, what had happened to Chittor, was determined never to submit to the Mughals, as all other Rajput rulers meanwhile had done, and to regain Chittor. Akbar first tried to make a treaty with Pratap, because he was aware of the difficulties of a battle in the hilly region of the Aravalli hills. He sent emissaries four times to Pratap. Pratap, who needed some time to consolidate his army and make his preparations for the inevitable battles, was clever enough to adopt a delaying policy for sometime.

When Akbar sent Man Singh of Amber as his negotiator, it brought about a showdown between the two men. Pratap, who despised Man Singh, insulted the latter by refusing to share the dinner with him. This led to the Battle of Haldighati. Meanwhile Pratap was prepared not only for the battle, because he had received the treasures from his Prime Minister and had won the support of the chieftain of the Bhils, Rana Punja, and his men, but he also was prepared, in the eventuality of not winning the battle, for a guerrilla war.

The Battle of Haldighati was fought on 21st June 1576. About 500 warriors died both sides. Pratap himself was seriously wounded, as also his famous horse Chetak. A faithful and brave follower of Pratap, Jhala Man, sacrificed his life for Pratap. When he noticed the situation and the danger for his king, he quickly took the royal umbrella and the other royal insignias and irritated the Mughals, who pursued him instead of Pratap. The brave stallion Chetak fled with his beloved master on his back into the hills, until he had reached a safe place in a valley. Then Chetak died. Today there is a special Chetak Memorial in that place to visit.

Neither side had won either the battle or the war. All further trials of Akbar to beat Pratap were finally without success. After a last attack in AD 1584 Akbar gave up his pursuit of Pratap.

The great hero Maharana Pratap Singh died on 19th January 1597 at Chawand. Despite his restless military activities he had eleven wives and 17 sons, of whom the eldest, Amar Singh (AD 1597-1620), succeeded to the throne.

Mughal historians record the extraordinary happening, that Akbar had tears of mourning when he heard about the death of his great enemy. Dursa Adha, a famous poet in Akbar's court, recited a couplet, which in translation is:

The Great Freedom Fighter Maharana Pratap (1572-1597)

> Guhilot Rana, you have won even in death, because on hearing of your demise the emperor was silent, bit his tongue, sighed, and tears welled up in his eyes. O! Pratap! You kept your horses unbranded, your head unbowed, your fame untarnished, you were strong enough, to carry on your work against heavy odds. You never participated in Naurozza Festival, nor did you mount guard on the Imperial presence, down the jharokha darshan.You attained a very high place in this world. On hearing of your death, O! Pratap! Akbar's eyes were dimmed and his tongue stuck in his throat.

From Akbar's side it must have been a relation of love and hate.

Colonel Tod writes that Akbar died on the midnight of 25th-26th October 1605 after three weeks of suffering. As Tod records he shall have tried to poison Raja Man Singh on 3rd October 1605 with prepared *ma'ajum*, but had mistakenly consumed a part of the poison himself.

After the last sacking of Chittor, the Maharanas of Mewar established their capital at Udaipur, the dreamlike city of lakes often called 'The City of Sunrise' or 'The Venice of Asia'.

View of Udaipur and the Palaces

A Tour Of Chittor

As already mentioned in previous chapter, the fort of Chittor is situated on a 170 m high table hill, about 450 m above sea level, with deep declivities on all sides and surrounded by 13 km of battlements. The narrow hill has an extension from the north to the south of almost 5 km. It is very narrow from west to east. It measures 280 ha.

Inside the mostly ruined citadel were beautiful palaces, wonderful temples in finest Hindu and Jain architecture, colleges, bazaars, tanks, and lakes, including mountain springs, until the *sakka* in 1567. Much of the former grandeur may still be seen today. The two hours' trip from Udaipur on a very good and fast road is a most worthwhile journey.

View to the Ramparts

One of the Gates of Chittor

Chittor can only be entered by two sides, the main entrance in the west and the Suraj Pol in the east. The main way to the fort leads you through seven *pols* (gates):Padal Pol, Bhairon Pol, Hanuman Pol, Ganesha Pol, Jodla Pol, Laxman Pol, and Ram Pol. The Ram Pol is the main entrance to the fort. At the Padal Pol a tablet remembers Prince Bagh Singh of Deodia who fell here in AD 1535 during the second sack of Chittor (attack of Bahadur Shah of Gujarat).

Close to the Bhairan Pol, the young hero Jaimal Rathore of Badnor was finally killed during the attack of the Great Mughal Akbar, supported by the Raja of Amber in 1567. The *chattris* are erected in memory of Jaimal and his clansman Patta of Kailwa. In front of the Ram Pol you will see two other *chattris*. They are a memoriam to the other young hero of the third *sakka* of Chittor, Patta, his bride, and his mother. There is an opening through which traitors and criminals would have been thrown out in former times.

When you turn after the Ram Pol to your right, you will see, after a few meters on the left side, Banbir's wall, which Banbir constructed for his defence against the real Maharana Udai Singh.

Very close on the same side is the Shringar Chawri, a temple built around AD 1448 by the treasurer of Maharana Kumbha opposite to the huge palace of Maharana Kumbha (AD 1433-68). Originally, here was a palace of the first Maharana of Mewar, Maharana Hamir. The great Kumbha made enormous additions to the original palace. It is a three-storeyed building with two wings.

Though, only ruins are left now, this palace gives you a good idea of the beauty of Rajput architecture at Kumbha's time and his taste. In this palace, the founder of Udaipur, Maharana Udai Singh, was born, and in the *Zenana* lived the famous poetess Mira Bai.

You enter the palace on the east through the Tripolia, a gate with octagonal towers, crowned by domes and you reach a large courtyard. Here you can see the former stables and the *sabha*. A long passageway connects the courtyard with the private suites

Banbir's Wall

Shringar Chawri

Palace of Maharana Kumbha

of the palace, situated at different levels. The apartments of the Kanwar Pade (heir apparent) in the south-west corner are in the best condition. Fragments of blue tilework indicate that the palace was once decorated with blue tiles. This palace is a great masterpiece of Hindu architecture of the fifteenth century.

There is an underground entrance through which it is said that the beautiful Rani Padmini led all the noble women and children into the cellar to perform the *jauhar*. Very interesting, too, is that, the palace has — like the City Palace in Udaipur — a Badi Pol and a Tripolia Pol. It may be that the Maharanas of Mewar thought of constructing some buildings in Udaipur like they had in Chittor, the sacked capital. From the walls of the massive ramparts you can have a nice view over the new Chittor, lying to the fort of the hill, painted blue, like the city of Jodhpur.

When you continue the road to the east, you will come to the beautiful Fateh Prakash Palace, built by Maharana Fateh Singh (AD 1884-1930), who in 1920s did a lot of restoration works, in Chtittor as well as in Kumbhalgarh. The Fateh Prakash Palace, formerly the private residence of Maharana Fateh in Chittor, houses an archaeological museum and a college today. There is

Inside of Kumbha's Palace

Inside View of Kumbha's Palace

also the beautiful temple area of Jain temples Sat Bis Dewari. These temples remind very much of famous Jain temples of Ranakpur, which are close to the fort of Kumbhalgarh, built by the Prime minister of Maharana Kumbha. The temples contain 27 shrines. The marble carvings are most beautiful.

When you leave the main temple and turn left, 'Meera'), the daughter-in-

Detail of the Palace

View of Chittor from Kumbha's Palace

Jain temple in Chittor

The Jain Temples

Detail of the Jain Temple

View from the Jain Temples to Fateh Prakash Palace

श्री मीरा मन्दिर

in the south direction, you reach the temples of Kumbha Shyamji and Mira Bai Temple. The Kumbha Shyamji Temple was built by Maharana Kumbha in AD 1448 and is dedicated to Varaha (boar), an incarnation of Lord Vishnu. The Mira Bai Temple is dedicated to the princely poetess Mira Bai (often also written 'Meera'), the daughter-in-law of the Mighty Sanga, who had devoted her life to Lord Krishna. In front of the temple is a *chattri* in memory of Rai Das of Banaras, the spiritual leader of Mira Bai.

Next to visit is the important Samideshwar Temple, which was built in the eleventh century and renovated by Maharana Mokal (AD 1421-33), the father of the Great Kumbha in AD 1428. Therefore, the temple is also called Mokalji Temple. The sanctum contains a *Shivalinga* and a beautiful, huge icon of Lord Shiva in black stone (tri-idol).

Very close is the Mahasati, the place, encircled by walls, where Rani Karnawati, the widow of the Mighty Sanga and mother of Maharana Udai Singh, performed the second *jauhar* in AD 1535 with all other noble Rajput women, girls, and children.

Samideshwar Temple

Palace of Padmini

Padmini's Pavilion

The Mahasati has two gates. When you leave through the southern gate and descend a long winding flight of steps, you reach Gaumukh Kund, a cow-mouthed water reservoir. Here Hindus take a sacred bath.

On your way to the south you pass the Jaimal-Patta lake, named after the two young heroes, who defended Chittor against the attack of the united forces of Akbar and the Raja of Amber, which ended with the third *sakka* and *jauhar* in AD 1567.

The Mardana

The next important place to visit is the palace of Rani Padmini. The original palace must have been destroyed. Some historians say that this palace was re-constructed in the nineteenth century. Inside the *Mardana* you can see a room which is opposite to the water-pavilion and where there are two mirrors, in which you can see the steps of the pavilion. This is how Ala-ud Din would have seen Padmini — by spotting her reflection in the mirrors of the *Mardana*.

Not far away is the palace of Jaimal and Patta. You can still see traces of beautiful decorations with coloured tiles that existed formerly.

Kalika Mata Temple

Palace of Jaimal and Patta

A little to the south you will find the Kalika Mata Temple. It is suggested by some historians, to be the oldest building of Chittor. Originally, it was a Surya Mandir, dedicated to the Sun God, which was built by Bapa Rawal. After its destruction by Muslim invaders, it was rebuilt by Maharana Hamir and dedicated to the goddess Kali (Kalika). This large temple has beautiful stone carvings on the pillars, the roof, and in the interior. It is still a centre of pilgrimage for Hindus from near and far.

If you follow the road farther to the south, you can go to the southern end of the hill, called Chittori Burj, or you can turn to the north. On your way north you reach Rajtila, a high raised platform, where during the rule of the Mauryas (the rulers before Bapa Rawal were elected as kings of Chittor) coronation ceremonies shall have been performed.

When you continue on the road to the north, two domes can be seen from the road, which are called the Domes of Gora and Badal (the uncle and cousin of Padmini).

Now, you reach the beautiful Bhimlat Kund, which is associated with the famous Bhim of the *Mahabharata*. Today, you can see children enjoying the refreshment of the water in this beautiful tank.

When you go on, you will find on the left side of the street a beautiful temple, named Adbuji Temple. This temple was built by Maharana Raimal (AD 1473-1509). The exterior of the temple shows delicate carvings and inside is a huge icon of Lord Shiva.

View from Rajtila

Bhimlat Kund

Details of Adbuji Temple

Previous page: Adbuji Temple

Suraj Pol

The Suraj Pol from Outside

Ratan Singh's Palace and Ratneshwar Kund

Kirti Stambha and Mahavir Swami Temple

From this place you have a wonderful view over Chittor, to the famous Vijaya Stambha, and to the only gate to the east, the Suraj Pol, which lies opposite to the Adbuji Temple.

Some historians believe that Rana Ratan had escorted his 'enemy guest' Ala-ud Din through this gate and was kidnapped there. Just near the gate is a monument in honour of Chundawat Sardar Rawat Sai Das, who died here in the battle with Akbar in AD 1567. Not far from here, you'll find one of the two impressive towers of Chittor, the Kirti Stambha (tower of fame). This tower is dedicated to Shri Adinath Rishabhdeo, the first Jain *tirthankara* (enlightened soul), which is smaller than the Vijaya Stambha. It was built in the twelfth century by a rich Jain. It is 24 m high and has seven storeys with 54 steps. Each storey is different from the other in the beautiful carvings and ornaments of the Jain idols. This tower was repaired by Maharana Fateh Singh (AD 1884-30).

As you can see, the Mahavir Swami Temple is very close to the Kirti Stambha. This temple has no idol.

When you continue your way to the north, you will reach the Lakhotapol or Lakhotabari. Now, you turn to the south and you will reach another most beautiful place, the Kukreshwar Kund with Kukreshwar Mahadev temple and the palace of Maharana Ratan Singh (AD 1527-31). You might remember that he was the immediate successor of the Mighty Sanga and the elder step brother of Vikramaditya and Udai. Some historians record that Maharana Udai Singh lived in this palace until he left Chittor with his family before the attack of Akbar.

When you go on, you pass through an area with small houses. Now you again reach Fateh Prakash Palace and then come to the impressive Vijaya Stambha (tower of victory). Some historians report that this tower was built by Maharana Kumbha in commemoration of his great victory and triumph over the ruler of Malwa, Mahmud Khalji in AD 1440. Numerous sculptures elaborately decorate the exterior of the tower. It is 36.5 m (120 ft) high and has nine storeys, served by a narrow stairway. It is

Kirti Stambha

Vijaya Stambha

covered from top to bottom with delicate carvings in red sandstone and white marble, depicting the social life of that time. When you climb up the 157 steps, you have a wonderful view of Chittor and the surrounding plains.

In front of this tower is a beautiful gate with delightful sculptures.

Now, our tour is at its end. If you want to know more about

the unique history of the world's oldest ruling dynasty, you can read the book: *The Kingdom of Mewar: Great Struggles and Glory of the World's Oldest Ruling Dynasty*.

Here you will get more detailed information about the rulers of Mewar from early times until the days of the recent custodian of the House of Mewar, Maharana Arvind Singh Mewar. It is a very enlivening account of Mewar's history with plenty of photographs.

जोद्रढराखेधरमको ताहीराखेकरतार

Historical-Genealogical Tree of the Dynasty of the Maharanas of Mewar

1.	Guhil (Guhdatt)	AD 566-586
2.	Bhoj	AD 586-606
3.	Mahendra I	AD 606-626
4.	Nag (Nagaditya)	AD 626-646
5.	Shiladitya	AD 646-661
6.	Aparajit	AD 661-688
7.	Mahendra II	AD 688-734
8.	Kalbhoj (Bapa Rawal) (The real founder of Mewar)	AD 734-753
9.	Khuman I	AD 753-773
10.	Mattat	AD 773-793
11.	Bhartri Bhatt	AD 793-813
12.	Sinha	AD 813-828
13.	Khuman II	AD 828-853
14.	Mahayak	AD 853-878
15.	Khuman III	AD 878-942
16.	Bhartri Bhatt II	AD 942-943
17.	Allat	AD 951-953

18.	Narwahan	AD 971-973
19.	Shaliwahan	AD 973-977
20.	Shakti Kumar	AD 977-993
21.	Amba Prasad	AD 993-1007
22.	Shuchi Varma	AD 1007-1021
23.	Nar Varma	AD 1021-1035
24.	Keerti Varma	AD 1035-1051
25.	Yograj	AD 1051-1068
26.	Vairath	AD 1068-1088
27.	Hanspal	AD 1088-1103
28.	Vair Singh	AD 1103-1107
29.	Vijai Singh	AD 1107-1127
30.	Ari Singh I	AD 1127-1138
31.	Chaud Singh	AD 1138-1148
32.	Vikram Singh	AD 1148-1158
33.	Ran Singh	AD 1158-1168
34.	Kshem Singh	AD 1168-1172
35.	Samant Singh	AD 1172-1179
36.	Kumar Singh	AD 1179-1191
37.	Mathan Singh	AD 1191-1211
38.	Padam Singh	AD 1211-1213
39.	Jaitra Singh	AD 1213-1253
40.	Tej Singh	AD 1261-1267
41.	Samar Singh I	AD 1273-1302
42.	Ratan Singh I (Husband of Padmini)	AD 1302-1303
43.	Hamir (Hameer) Singh I (1st to be called Maharana)	AD 1326-1364
44.	Kheta Singh	AD 1366-1382

45.	Lakha	AD 1382-1421
46.	Mokal	AD 1421-1433
47.	Kumbha (The Great Kumbha)	AD 1433-1468
48.	Udai Singh I	AD 1468-1473
49.	Raimal	AD 1473-1509
50.	Sangram Singh I (The Mighty Sanga)	AD 1509-1527
51.	Ratan Singh II	AD 1527-1531
52.	Vikramaditya Singh	AD 1531-1536
53.	Udai Singh II (The founder of Udaipur)	AD 1537-1572
54.	Pratap Singh I	AD 1572-1597
55.	Amar Singh I	AD 1597-1620
56.	Karan Singh (The builder of Jag Mandir)	AD 1620-1628
57.	Jagat Singh I (The builder of Jagdish Temple)	AD 1628-1652
58.	Raj Singh I	AD 1653-1680
59.	Jai Singh I	AD 1680-1698
60.	Amar Singh II	AD 1698-1710
61.	Sangram Singh II	AD 1710-1734
62.	Jagat Singh II (The builder of Jag Niwas)	AD 1734-1751
63.	Pratap Singh II	AD 1751-1753
64.	Raj Singh II	AD 1754-1761
65.	Ari Singh II	AD 1761-1773
66.	Hamir Singh II	AD 1773-1778
67.	Bhim (Bheem) Singh	AD 1778-1828
68.	Jawan Singh	AD 1828-1838

69.	Sardar Singh	AD 1838-1842
70.	Swarup (Swaroop) Singh	AD 1842-1861
71.	Shambhu Singh	AD 1861-1874
72.	Sajjan Singh	AD 1874-1884
73.	Fateh Singh (The light of the Hindus)	AD 1884-1930
74.	Bhupal Singh (The last independent ruler)	AD 1931-1955
75.	Bhagwat Singh Mewar	AD 1955-1984
76.	Arvind Singh Mewar	AD 1984-

Glossary

Agni – Fire god

Agni-upasi Suryavansi – sun born fire-worshippers

Amba Mataji – Mother Goddess

Ankus – elephant goat

Aranyavaini Devi temple – temple of the goddess of the forest

Arya (Aryans) – Aria

Badi Mahal – garden palace, large garden pavilion

Badi Pol – main gate of the Palace

bagh – garden

Baghela Karna – queen of the clan of Baghela

Bahadur – brave, champion, hero

Bapa – father

Bara Mahal – great palace

Bari – a special servant

Brahmin – member of the Indian priestly class

Bund – embankment, dam

Chandra – moon

Chandra Mahal – moon palace

Chattri – pavilion with dome; also tomb monument

Chowk – courtyard

Chundawats – nobles (sub-clan) of Mewar, descendants of Chunda, eldest son of Maharana Lakha

Darbar or *durbar* – Indian royal assembly; royal audience

Daulat khana – treasury

Deepdan – lighting of the lamp

Devi – female goddess

Dharam sabha – committee for religious affairs

Dharma – moral and religious duty; also religion

Dhol – drum

Dhola Mahal – white palace

Dholi – drummer

Diwan – Prime Minister to an Indian ruler

Diwan khana – drawing room

Durbar – see: *darbar*

Gadi or *gaddi* – princely throne or the cushion on the throne

Ganesh, Ganesha – Elephant god, son of Shiva and Parvati, god of good luck

Garh – fort or fortification

Ghat – steps to a bathing place (lake or river)

Hatyaro – murderer

Haveli – large town house or mansion of a noble or also of merchants

Howdah – palanquin on elephant

Jai – victory *Jai* or *Jaya*

Stambha – tower of victory

Jaggat Gur – guardian of mankind

Jagir – an assignment of land

Jagirdar – holder of a *jagir,* an assignment of land

Jauhar – voluntary self-immolation in a funeral pyre of woman and children

Kanwar – prince (when used as prefix) or princess (when used as suffix)

Khas Odi – chief shooting lodge

Kawrani Sahiba – title of a Maharani

Ki – of

Krishna – eighth incarnation of Vishnu

Kumari – princess

Kund – water-reservoir, tank

Lakshmi or *Laxmi* – wife of god Vishnu, a goddess of wealth and beauty

Lakulish Cult – a religious order, comparable to the Christian catechism

Linga (*lingam*) – phallic emblem of Shiva

Magri – hill

Maha – great

Mahal – a palace

Maharaja – Rajput king

Maharaj Kumar – great prince

Maharana – 'King of Kings' under the Rajput rulers, the title of only the rulers of Mewar/ Udaipur

Maharani – Rajput queen

Mandir – palace or temple

Manzil – residence; tower

Mardana – men's quarters of a palace

Moti – pearl

Moti Magri – pearl-hill

Murti – images of gods and goddesses

Nagara – kettledrum

Nawab – Muslim ruler, originally 'deputy' to the Mughal Emperor, later a virtually independent prince

Niwas (*nivas*) – palace

Parvati – goddess, the wife of Lord Shiva

Pathan – pagan

Pol – gate

Prarthana – prayers

Puja – worship for god; prayer ceremonies

Purdah – seclusion or screen to prevent women being seen by strangers

Rana – short form of the title of the rulers of Mewar

Raja – ruling king

Raj Kumar – Rajput prince

Rajput – warrior caste; literally 'Sons of Kings'

Sabha – assembly hall

Sagar – artificial lake

Sardar – Rajput chieftain, a leading nobleman in the court of a Rajput king

Sati (satee) – ritual self-immolation of widows on their husband's funeral pyres

Shah – title of a Persian or an Islamic king

Shree (Shri) – term to address a most honourable being

Shri Eklingji – Shiva as deity at the temple of Eklingji

Shriji – a special term for the Maharana of Mewar

Stambha – pillar; tower

Suraj – sun

Thakur – Rajput fief-holder or baron

Tika – ceremonial or festival mark on the forehead

Tilaka – mark made on the forehead of the king at the time of coronation

Tripolia – triple arched ceremonial gate

Vakil – agent; attorney; ambassador

Vilas – palace

Vishnu – a god, the preserver of the universe and second divinity in the Hindu Triad

Zamindar – landholder

Zenana – women's quarters in the palace

Sources and Bibliography

I. MEWAR

Bedi, Anju: *And Battles Passed Below*, Kumbhalgarh.

Davenport, Hugh: *The Trials & Triumphs of the Mewar Kingdom*, Udaipur (1975).

Erskine, K.D.: *Rajputana Gazetteers* - Vol. II-A & Vol. II-B, The Mewar Residency [Published: 1908, 1st rpt. 1992].

Goyal, Suresh: *The Invincible Maharana Pratap* (1983).

Masters, Brian: *Maharana – The Story of the Rulers of Udaipur* (1990).

Mathur, P.K.: *Costumes of the Rulers of Mewar* (1994).

Mathur, T.K.: *Feudal Polity in Mewar* (1987).

Mehta, Jodh Singh: *Abu to Udaipur* (1994).

Mewar, Arvind Singh: *Inheritance 76* (1996).

Mukta, Parita: *Upholding the Common Life – The Community of Mirabai* (1994).

Nath, R.: *Antiquities of Chittorgadh* (1984).

Payne, C.H.: *Tod's Annals of Rajasthan, The Annals of Mewar* (1960).

Pinhey, Lt. Col. A.F.: *History of Mewar* [1st published 1909, 1st rpt, 1996].

Rathore, L.S.: *Maharana Hammir of Mewar – Chitor's Lost Freedom Restored* (1991).

Sansthan, Sahitya: *Mewar through the Ages* (1969).

Sharma, G.N.: *Glories of Mewar.*

Sharma, G.N.: *Haqiqat Bahida – 1, H.I.H. Maharana Fateh Singhji of Udaipur* (1992).

Sharma, G.N; Mathur, M.N. *et al.*: *Maharana Pratap And His Times – Rajat Jayanti Souvenir* (1989).

Singh, Kesri: *The Hero of Haldighati* (1996).

Somani, R.V.: *History of Mewar* (1976).

Somani, R.V.: *Later Mewar* (1985).

Somani, R.V.: *Maharana Kumbha and His Times* (1995).

Tod, Col. James: *Annals and Antiquities of Rajasthan,* 3 volumes [1920, rpt. 1993].

II. RAJASTHAN

A. English

Ahuja, D.R.: *Folklore of Rajasthan* (1980).

Beach, Milo Cleveland: *Rajput Painting at Bundi and Kota* (1994).

Bhattacharya, Sunanda: *Role of Jats and Rajputs in the Mughal Court* (1995).

Darda, R.S.: *Administration of Princely State* (1985).

Goetz, Hermann: *Rajput Art and Architecture*, ed. by Jyotindra Jain & Jutta Jain-Neubauer, (1978).

Hechenblaikner, Lois: *Rajasthan* (1995).

Joshi, Varsha: *Polygamy & Purdah – Women & Society among Rajputs* (1995).

Kathuria, R. P.: *Life in the Courts of Rajasthan* (1987).

Mehra, Sunil: *Rajasthan – An Enduring Romance* (1993).

Neumann-Adrian, Michael; Panagariya, B.L.; Pahariya, N.C.: *Political, Socio-Economic and Cultural History of Rajasthan* (1993).

Pande, Ram: *Painting as Source of Rajasthan History* (1985).

Ratnawat, Shyam Singh: *Rajput Nobility* (1989).

Schomer, Karine *et al.*: *The Idea of Rajasthan*, Vol. I: Constructions; Vol. II: Institutions (1994).

Singh, Dhananjaya: *The House of Marwar* (1994).

Singh, Kishore: *Rajasthan* (1995).

Singhi, N. K.; Joshi, Rajendra: *Folk, Faith & Feudalism* (1995).

Strasser: *Rajasthan/Gujarat* (1992).

Trevor, Col. G. H.: *Chiefs and Leading Families in Rajputana* [1st. published 1894, rpt. 1992].

Trevor, Col. G. H.: *Rhymes of Rajputana* [1st published 1894, rpt 1990].

Vashistha, R.K.: *Art And Artists of Rajasthan* (1985).

B. German

Höfer *et al.*: *Rajasthan* (1993), (APA-Guide).

Keilhauer, Anneliese & Peter: *Indiens Königsland Rajasthan* (1983).

Kreisel, *et al.*: *Rajasthan - Land der Könige* (1995).

Krüger, Hardy: *Indische Blätter in Hardy Krüger 'Weltenbummler – Reise zu Menschen Göttern'* (1994).

Molitor, Juliane Anna Lia: *Portraits in sechs Fürstenstaaten Rajasthans vom 17.bis 20.* Jahrhundert (1985).

Neumann-Adrian; Michael & Edda : *Rajasthan* (1995).

III. GENERAL

A. English

Abul-L-Fazl: *The Akbar Nama*, Vol. I, II, III, tr. by H. Beveridge [1st. published 1902-39, rpt. 1989, 1993].

Allen, Charles: *Lives of the Indian Princes* (1984).

Babur, Zahiruddin Muhammad: *Babur Nama (Memoirs of Babur)* tr. from the original Turki text by Annette Susannah Beveridge [1st. published 1921, 2nd rpt. 1995].

Beny/Menen: *India* (1969).

Dass, Diwan Jarmani: *Maharaja – Lives and Loves and Intrigues of Indian Princes* (1969).

Desai: *Gods, Guardians and Lovers – Temple Sculpture from Northern India* (1993).

Ehnbom,Daniel J.: *Indian Miniatures – the Ehrenfield Collection* (1985).

Guy, John: *Indian Art & Connoisseurship* [1995] - Essays In Honour Of Douglas Barrett.

Ions, Veronica: *Indian Mythology* (1983).

Majumdar *et al.*: *The History and Culture of the Indian People* (11 volumes):

Vol.1: The Vedic Age.

Vol.2: The Age of Imperial Unity.

Vol.3: The Classic Age.

Vol.4: The Age of Imperial Kanay

Vol.5: The Struggle for Empire.

Vol.6: The Delhi Sultanate.

Vol.7: The Mughul Empire.

Maury: *Folk Origins of Indian Art* (1969).

Michell, George; Martinelli, Antonio: *The Royal Palaces of India* (1994).

Pal/Kumar: *Court Paintings of India* (No. 319 of the limited edition) (1983).

Patnaik, Naveen: *A Second Paradise – Indian Courtly Life 1590 - 1947* (1985).

Paul, E. Jaiwant: *'By my Sword and Shield' – Traditional Weapons of the Indian Warrior* (1995).

Robinson, Andrew; Uchiyama, Sumio: *Maharaja* (1988).

Rousselet: *India of the Rajahs,* Limited Reprint (1985) of the original of '*India and his Native Princes*' (1882).

Sugich, Michael: *Palaces of India* (1992).

Tammita-Delgoda, Sinharaja: *A Traveller's History of India* (1994).

Tillotsen, G.H.R.: *Mughal India* (1991).

Vidyalankar, Pandit Satyakam: *The Holy Vedas* [1983, rpt. 1969].

Welch, Stuart Cary: *India: Art and Culture, 1300-1900* [1st published: 1985, rpt. 1997].

B. German

Alsdorf, Ludwig: *Indien* (1940).

Aubert: *Nordindien* (1994).

Babur, Zahiruddin Muhammad: *Die Erinnerungen des ersten Großmoguls von Indien – Das Babur-nama – übersetzt ins Deutsche vo Wolfgang Stammler auf Grundlage der französischen Übersetzung von Jean-Louis Bacqué-Grammont* (1989).

Barkemeier, Thomas: *Indien – Der Norden* (1994).

Chévrillon, André: *In Indien* (1911).

Doehring, E.T. *et al.*: *Indische Kunst* (1925).

Drunneberg, Erwin: *Von Ceylon zum Himalaja* (1926).

Ehlers, Otto E.: *An Indischen Fürstenhöfen*, 2 Vols. (1885).

Embree, Ainslie; Wilhelm, Friedrich: *Indien – Geschichte des Subkontinents von der Induskultur bis zum Beginn der englischen Herrschaft* (1992).

Franz, Heinrich Gerhard: *Das Alte Indien* (1990).

Glasenapp, Helmuth von: *Indien – Der indische Kulturkreis* (1925).

Härtel, Herbert; Boyer, Jeannine: *Indien und Südostasien – Propyläen Kunstgeschichte* (1985).

Hauswirth, Frieda: *Schleier vor Indiens Frauengemächern* (1935).

Hürlimann, Martin: *Indien – Baukunst, Landschaft und Volksleben* (1928).

Kühnel, Ernst: *Indische Miniaturen* (1937).

Kippling, Rudyard: *Lichtes und dunkles Indien* (1963).

Kreisel: *Indische Kultur* (1987).

Langer, Heinz; Rudolph, Manfred: *Indien* (1972).

Lessmann, S. *et al.*: *Geschichte des Alten Indiens* (1878).

Maeritz, Kay: *Indien* (1993).

Mayer, Adrian; Balocco, Patrizia: *Reise durch Indien* (1994).

Nobel, Alphons: *Tempel, Paläste und Dschungel* (1929).

Robinson; Uchiyama: *Maharadschas* (1988).

Tavernier, Jean Baptiste: *Reisen zu den Reichtümern Indiens – Abenteuerliche Jahre beim Großmoghul, 1641-1667* (1984).

Acknowledgements

I want to cordially express my deep gratitude to my friends, Maharana Arvind Singh Mewar and his wife, Vijayraj Kumari Mewar, for their generous hospitality during my stay in Udaipur and their support in every sense of my work.

I also wish to express my heart-felt gratitude to Shri Mohan Singhji Kothari for his great support. He provided me a lot of information for my very important informative book *The Kingdom of Mewar — Great Struggles and Glory of the World's Oldest Ruling Dynasty* and spent several hours in discussing details of the history of Mewar and working out the glossary with me. During the intensive and interesting work together, we became friends.

I have to specially thank him very much for making several corrections in the English edition of my guide on City Palace Museum Udaipur, as also in this guide on Chittor. I am indebted to Shri Bhupendra Singhji of Auwa for his great support.

I also wish to thank the whole staff of Shiv Niwas Palace Hotel, who kindly cared for me during my stay and read nearly each wish in my eyes, before I could tell it, especially Shri Ajay Singhji, the current manager of the Aodhi Hotel at Kumbhalgarh.

Last but not least I have to thank my dear son, Philipp Meininger, who supported me as much as possible in my every work.